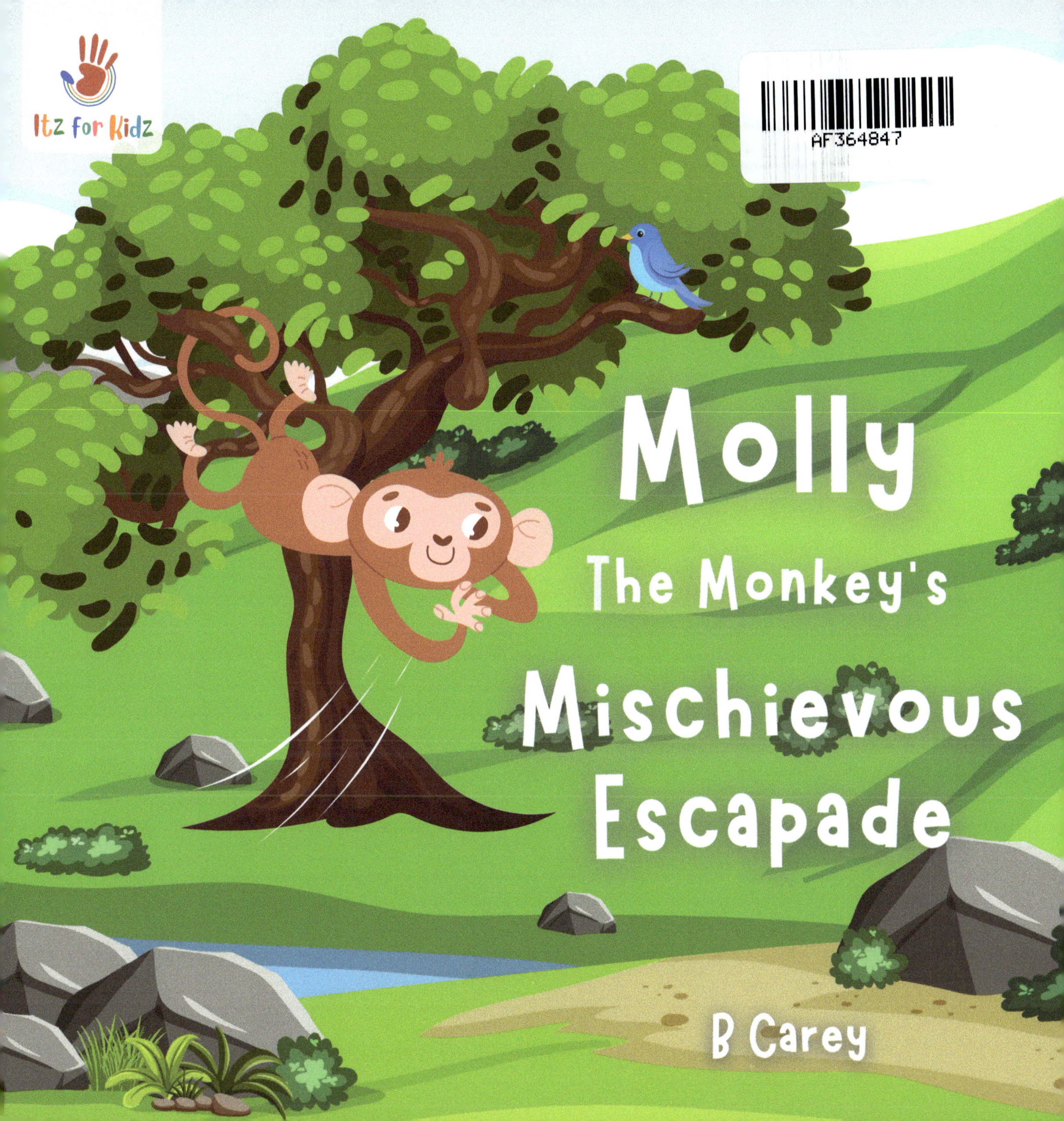

Itz for Kidz
Molly
The Monkey's
Mischievous
Escapade
B Carey

Molly the Monkey's Mischievous Escapade

ISBN : 978-81-977858-7-0

www.itzforkidz.com | hello@itzforkidz.com

Let's Begin....

"Be Happy."

Curiosity is wonderful, but always be kind
and responsible in your adventures.

"Be Happy."

—B Carey

www.ingramcontent.com/pod-product-compliance
Lightning Source LLC
LaVergne TN
LVHW071004180726

843512LV00017B/1289